CODING CONCEPTS
FOR KIDS

RANDY LYNN

CODING CONCEPTS FOR KIDS

Learn to Code Without a Computer

Illustration by Kristyna Baczynski

ROCKRIDGE PRESS

Thanks to my wife, Sissy, for encouraging me to take on the writing of this book, my son Daniel for reminding me to always strive for 100% plus extra credit, and my daughter Julia for inspiring me with her creativity and humor.

For general information on our other products and services or to obtain technical support, please contact our Customer Care Department within the United States at (866) 744-2665, or outside the United States at (510) 253-0500.

Rockridge Press publishes its books in a variety of electronic and print formats. Some content that appears in print may not be available in electronic books, and vice versa.

Interior and Cover Designer: Richard Tapp
Art Producer: Tom Hood
Editor: Jeanine Le Ny
Production Editor: Emily Sheehan
Illustration © Kristyna Baczynski, 2020

ISBN: Print 978-1-64739-235-2 | eBook 978-1-64739-236-9
R0

This book is dedicated to every child who dreams of creating something new, whether using code or any other tool. The world is yours.

Change it for the better.

CONTENTS

HELLO, CODERS!

Do you love using computers? You probably use one to play games, draw pictures, watch videos, read stories, or listen to music.

Computers can be a lot of fun, and you know what's even more fun? Using your creativity to invent something totally new! That's what coding is all about.

Learning how to code is a little like learning how to write. You can't write a book before you've learned your ABCs, right?

You can learn how to code on a computer, of course. But it's smart to begin learning without a computer. That's because being a great coder starts with being a great thinker.

This book will teach you some of the big ideas that young coders need to know. And there are lots of fun coding puzzles for you to do. This is the kind of book you can write in. In fact, I want you to write in it!

There are also activities you can do with friends or family. You'll have a chance to come up with coding games of your own, too.

CONGRATULATIONS!

You're the newest member of the Coder Crew, a team of kids who love to solve problems using code. The Coder Crew will be with you every step of the way.

AL: When you need step-by-step directions, you can count on Al. He has an amazing ability to take a tough problem and break it down into simple steps.

LO: Lo is the team's problem-solver. She knows how to think through a problem carefully to find the best solution.

PIXEL: Pixel is the Crew's creative expert. Need 10 different solutions to a challenge? She's your girl. Just don't call her "Pixie." She hates that.

DRAW YOUR PICTURE

YOUR NAME

BUG: He may be the youngest of the Crew, but Bug has his own special talents. He's great at spotting patterns and finding mistakes in code.

SPOT THE BOT: Spot is the Crew's robot dog. He is loyal and tends to get into a lot of trouble.

What are some of your best skills?

....

....

....

....

....

....

SO WHAT IS CODING, ANYWAY?

Computers are powerful tools that can do many different things. Computers work a little like our brains. They're really good at working with information, such as numbers and words.

Computers may seem really smart, but they can't think for themselves. That's why coders are so important. Coders write the instructions, or code, that tell computers what to do. These instructions are called programs, or apps. Without code, computers would be pretty useless.

Some simple apps have just a few lines of code. Others have thousands or even millions of lines of code. So, what can you do with all this code? Just about anything you can imagine. Code is a tool you can use to invent new things. It's like an artist's paintbrush, a sculptor's clay, a builder's bricks, or a writer's words.

Coders are also called "computer programmers."

HOW TO THINK LIKE A CODER

Learning to code is about teaching your brain to think in new ways. If you like to solve problems, do puzzles, play games, or come up with new ideas, you already have many of the skills you'll need to begin your coding journey. If not, don't worry. Thinking like a coder might seem a little tricky at first, but you can do it!

Here are some tips:

BREAK IT DOWN

Sometimes a problem seems hard just because it's so big.

Coders break down big problems by thinking of them as lots of little problems that can be solved one by one. That's a great skill to have in life—not just for coding, but for many other things.

Let's say you want to ride a bicycle without training wheels. How would you break down that challenge? You probably wouldn't start out by taking off the training wheels right away. Instead, you would work on some of the basic skills, one at a time, like keeping your balance, learning how to use the brakes, pedaling, and then eventually pedaling without the training wheels.

Riding a bike may just be one skill, but there are lots of little "parts" that work together. If a coding problem seems too hard, see if you can break the problem down and figure it out one step at a time.

LOOK FOR PATTERNS

A pattern is something that repeats over and over.

There are patterns all around us. Stripes, polka dots, and zigzags are common patterns used on clothes. But that's just one kind of pattern. You might follow a pattern every morning: wake up, get dressed, eat breakfast, and brush your teeth.

Where do you see patterns in your life?

Patterns are powerful! Coders look for patterns everywhere.

THINK LOGICALLY

Coders use logic to solve problems. What's logic? It's really just a way of thinking. Great problem-solvers come up with many different ways of doing something, and then decide on the smartest choice. Logical answers just make sense.

Should you start reading a new book on the last page? You could, of course, but that wouldn't be a logical thing to do.

In coding, like in everyday life, there can be many ways to do the same thing. But some ways are better (or more logical) than others.

CODER CREW CLUB RULES

Be creative. Use your imagination to solve problems and think up new ideas.

Dream big. You're never too young to come up with an idea that can change the world.

Keep learning. Learn something new every day. Before you know it, you'll be an expert.

Share ideas. Coding by yourself can be fun, but it's even better with friends.

Make mistakes. It's okay. Really! Mistakes don't mean you're a bad coder. They mean that you're trying out new ideas.

Don't give up. Stuck on a problem? Keep at it! And remember, it's okay to ask a friend or family member for help.

No matter what, have fun. That's what it's all about!

AWESOME ALGORITHMS

An algorithm is a set of instructions that are done step-by-step. Coders use algorithms to tell a computer what to do. Each step has to be clear and in the right order. That's because, although computers may be powerful, they can't think for themselves.

Did you know that you're already using algorithms every day? You wash your hands with soap and water and then dry them off. You follow a recipe to make cookies. You look both ways before crossing the street. These are just a few examples of algorithms.

To make a great algorithm:

1. *Include every single step.*
2. *Keep the steps in the right order.*
3. *Make each step super simple.*

ORDER UP!

CODE À LA MODE

Follow the algorithm below to help Lo get to her favorite food.

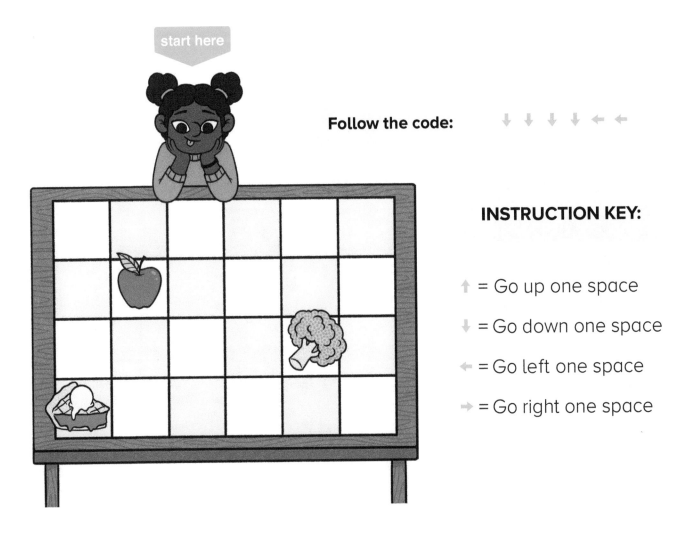

Follow the code: ↓ ↓ ↓ ↓ ← ←

INSTRUCTION KEY:

↑ = Go up one space

↓ = Go down one space

← = Go left one space

→ = Go right one space

WHAT IS LO'S FAVORITE FOOD?

_____

Coders call each instruction in their code a "command." The → arrow is a command that means move one step to the right.

CODEO RODEO

Oh, no! Al lost his cowboy hat. Write an algorithm to help him find it. Use the up, down, left, and right arrows.

INSTRUCTION KEY:

↑ = Go up one space   ← = Go left one space

↓ = Go down one space   → = Go right one space

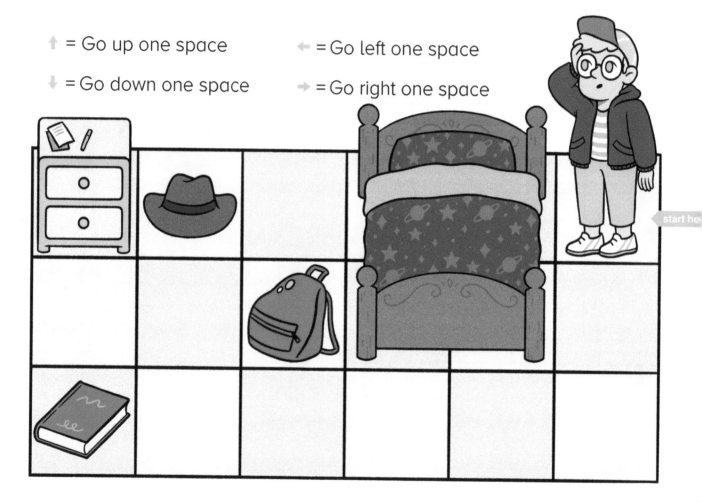

start here

WRITE YOUR ALGORITHM HERE USING ARROWS.

WORD SCRAMBLE

Can you unscramble the secret message? Follow the algorithm to move Lo, Bug, and Spot to the correct letters. Write each letter down as you complete the steps. The first one is done for you.

ALGORITHM   **LETTER**

D C R O E

→ →   C
→ → → →   ___
→   ___
→ → → → →   ___
→ → →   ___

E W C R

→ → →   ___
→ → → →   ___
→   ___
→ →   ___

K S R C O

→ → →   ___
→ → → → →   ___
→ → → →   ___
→   ___
→ →   ___

YOUR ANSWER:

C _ _ _ _ _   _ _ _ _   _ _ _ _ _ _ !

DRESS MESS

Uh, oh. Bug is having trouble getting ready this morning. Can you help him choose the correct algorithm for getting dressed?

Algorithm 1

PUT ON PANTS
PUT ON SHIRT
PUT ON UNDERWEAR
PUT ON UNDERSHIRT
PUT ON SOCKS

Algorithm 2

PUT ON SOCKS
PUT ON SHIRT
PUT ON UNDERSHIRT
PUT ON PANTS
PUT ON UNDERWEAR

Algorithm 3

PUT ON SOCKS
PUT ON UNDERWEAR
PUT ON PANTS
PUT ON UNDERSHIRT
PUT ON SHIRT

THE CORRECT ALGORITHM IS:

_____ .

It's super important to put code in the logical order. If you don't, you may be in for a surprise!

CODE CONNECT

Bug loves shapes and patterns. Use his algorithm to connect the dots and find out what the pattern is.

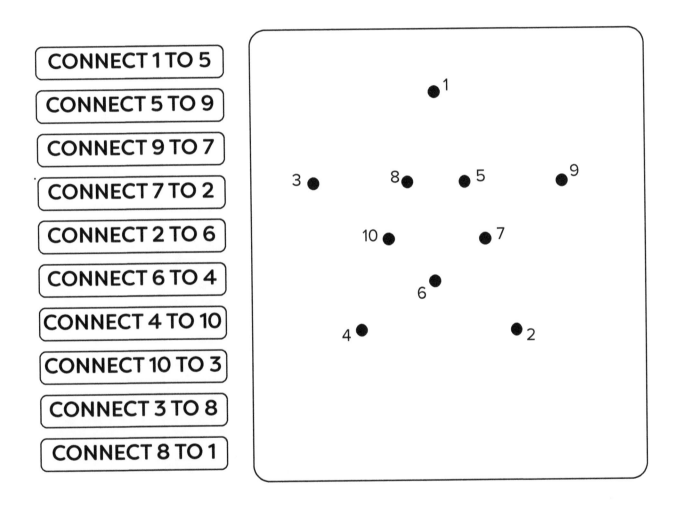

CONNECT 1 TO 5

CONNECT 5 TO 9

CONNECT 9 TO 7

CONNECT 7 TO 2

CONNECT 2 TO 6

CONNECT 6 TO 4

CONNECT 4 TO 10

CONNECT 10 TO 3

CONNECT 3 TO 8

CONNECT 8 TO 1

WHAT SHAPE DO YOU SEE?

TREASURE QUEST

Searching for hidden treasure is fun. But it's even better when you use an algorithm to guide your pirate friends to the treasure!

What You Need:

"Treasure," such as candy or a small toy
Blank sheet of paper
Pencil, pen, or crayon
Index cards (1 card for every step of your algorithm)

What You Do:

1. Hide the treasure somewhere in your house or yard.
2. On the blank sheet of paper, write "Start Here" and draw an arrow to show which way your friend should be facing when the hunt begins. Place it on the floor and be sure the arrow is pointing in the correct direction.
3. Next, create an algorithm. Write one arrow (↑, ↓, ←, or →) on each index card. Each card represents 1 step. For example, if you want your friend to take 10 steps forward, you would have 10 cards with the ↑ arrow.
4. Now give the stack of cards to your friend. Have them stand on top of the "Start Here" paper and then see if they can find the treasure.

It's a good idea to test your algorithm a few times before you start the game.

Pig Latin is a word game you can play with your friends. It's called "pig Latin" because it sounds a little like Latin, a very old language once spoken around the world.

Here's the algorithm for changing a word to pig Latin:

- Take the first letter and move it to the end of the word.
- Add "ay."

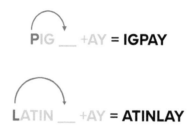

So, "My cat likes pickles" would be "Ymay atcay ikeslay icklespay" in pig Latin.

Try writing a message to a friend, and then use the algorithm to translate the message into pig Latin.

Now that you know what algorithms are all about, use this space to write your own. Try this idea first:

Write an algorithm for drawing a simple picture, such as a snowman or a house. Then ask a friend to follow it. Did the picture turn out like you thought it would?

Write another algorithm idea here:

LOTS OF LOOPS

Coders use loops when they want to repeat something.

Let's say you want to tell a robot to move forward by taking 100 steps. Imagine how long it would take you to write "move forward" 100 times! Instead, coders can put a loop around the instruction and tell the computer how many times to repeat a step. This is called a counting loop. So, to tell a robot to take 100 steps forward, you could tell it:

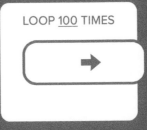

Once the robot takes 100 steps forward, it stops. If you wanted the robot to keep taking steps, you could even code the loop to never stop. That's called an infinite loop.

INFINITE PEPPERONI

RUN THE CODE

Bug and Spot are in a race. Bug takes one step forward, looped nine times. Spot takes two steps forward, looped four times. Who will make it past the finish line?

BUG'S CODE

LOOP <u>9</u> TIMES

➡️

SPOT'S CODE

LOOP <u>4</u> TIMES

➡️

➡️

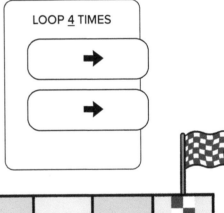

WHO FINISHED THE RACE?

LAUGH-A-LOOP

Rewrite the joke below using loops. How many times do you need to loop to tell the full joke?

Knock, knock.

Who's there?

Banana.

Banana who?

Knock, knock.

Who's there?

Banana.

Banana who?

Knock, knock.

Who's there?

Banana.

Banana who?

Knock, knock.

Who's there?

Orange.

Orange who?

Orange you glad I didn't say banana!

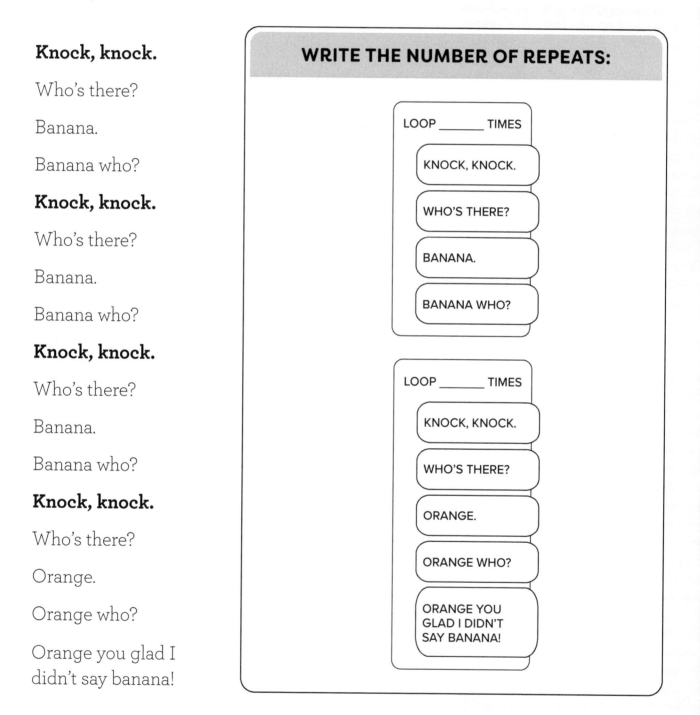

WRITE THE NUMBER OF REPEATS:

LOOP _____ TIMES

KNOCK, KNOCK.

WHO'S THERE?

BANANA.

BANANA WHO?

LOOP _____ TIMES

KNOCK, KNOCK.

WHO'S THERE?

ORANGE.

ORANGE WHO?

ORANGE YOU GLAD I DIDN'T SAY BANANA!

HIDDEN TOYS

Spot the Bot needs some help. Fill in the algorithm below. Tell Spot how many times to loop the code so he can find his toys.

GET BONE

LOOP _____ TIMES

← (left arrow)

↑ (up arrow)

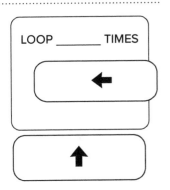

GET BALL

↑ (up arrow)

LOOP _____ TIMES

→ (right arrow)

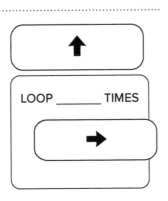

GET TEDDY BEAR

LOOP _____ TIMES

→ (right arrow)

LOOP _____ TIMES

↓ (down arrow)

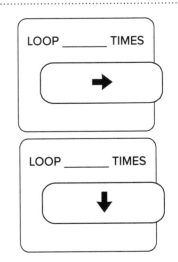

LAWN LOOPS

It's a hot day! Help Al mow his backyard and get to his tall glass of lemonade. Fill in the number of times each loop repeats.

LOOP _____ TIMES
→

LOOP _____ TIMES
↑

LOOP _____ TIMES
←

↓

LOOP _____ TIMES
→

STREET REPEAT

Most of the time, you want loops to repeat a few times and then stop. But some things, like traffic lights, loop forever.

Traffic lights follow the pattern of: stop, caution, go. Fill in the colors in the algorithm below to show the pattern.

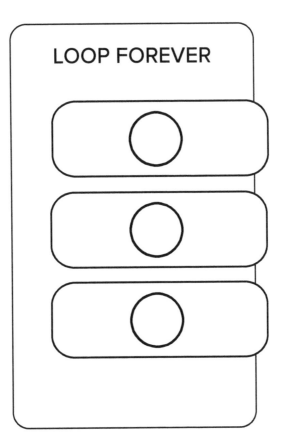

WHY WOULD WE WANT A TRAFFIC LIGHT TO LOOP FOREVER?

ALGO RHYTHM

Drum patterns are a special kind of musical algorithm. You don't even need a set of drums to play a pattern. Pots and pans work great!

Kitchen percussion is a lot of fun, but it can be loud. Be sure to let your parents know what you're doing first. And make sure nobody's sleeping!

What You Need:

Large pot
Skillet
2 spoons
Anything else that makes a cool sound

What You Do:

1. Place the pot and skillet "drums" in front of you with the pot on the left and the skillet on the right.

2. Count to four, slowly, as you hit the pot and pan with your spoons. Follow the musical algorithm by hitting the pot as you say "one" and the skillet as you say "two," and so on. When you reach four, repeat the pattern again, starting over from the beginning. Loop the whole pattern at least four times.

	1	2	3	4
Pot (Left Hand)	●		●	
Skillet (Right Hand)		●		●

3. This time, try hitting the pot twice when you count 3. Don't forget to repeat the pattern after you get to 4.

	1	2	3	4
Pot (Left Hand)	●		●●	
Skillet (Right Hand)		●		·

4. How would you play this one?

	1	2	3	4
Pot (Left Hand)	●		●●	
Skillet (Right Hand)		●●		●●

5. Now try writing your own pattern. What pattern sounds best to you? Would different kinds of pots and pans sound better?

	1	2	3	4

LOOPERCISE

Here's a fun idea you can do outdoors. Take some sidewalk chalk and design your own exercise course on your sidewalk, driveway, or another area where you can play safely.

Write the name of an exercise on the ground and the number of times it should be looped. Then add a second area with a different exercise and its number of repeats. Try to come up with at least four different activities.

Here's an example to help you come up with your very own exercise course.

Now that you know what looping is all about, use this space to write your own idea. Try this one first:

Come up with some cool dance moves, and loop each move a few times. Write down the code for your new looped dance routine, and then teach it to a friend!

Write your looping idea here.

CREATIVE CONDITIONALS

The word *conditional* means something that happens only if something else happens.

For example, if it's raining outside, then you use an umbrella. If you're tired, then you go to bed. If you're hungry, then you eat. Do you notice a pattern? If _____, then _____.

Coders use conditionals when they want one thing to happen if another thing happens first. Any time you want to code something that fits the "if/then" pattern, you'll use a conditional.

COOKIE CONDITIONS

EMOJI CODE

Follow the conditionals. Think about each if/then statement and decide if it's true or false. Then do what the code says.

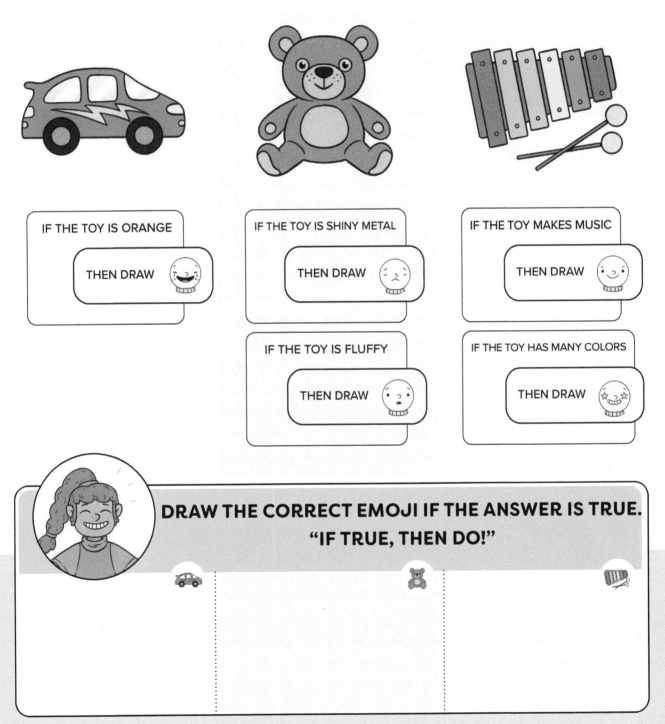

IF THE TOY IS ORANGE

THEN DRAW

IF THE TOY IS SHINY METAL

THEN DRAW

IF THE TOY MAKES MUSIC

THEN DRAW

IF THE TOY IS FLUFFY

THEN DRAW

IF THE TOY HAS MANY COLORS

THEN DRAW

**DRAW THE CORRECT EMOJI IF THE ANSWER IS TRUE.
"IF TRUE, THEN DO!"**

NAME GAMES

Help name these animal friends using conditionals.

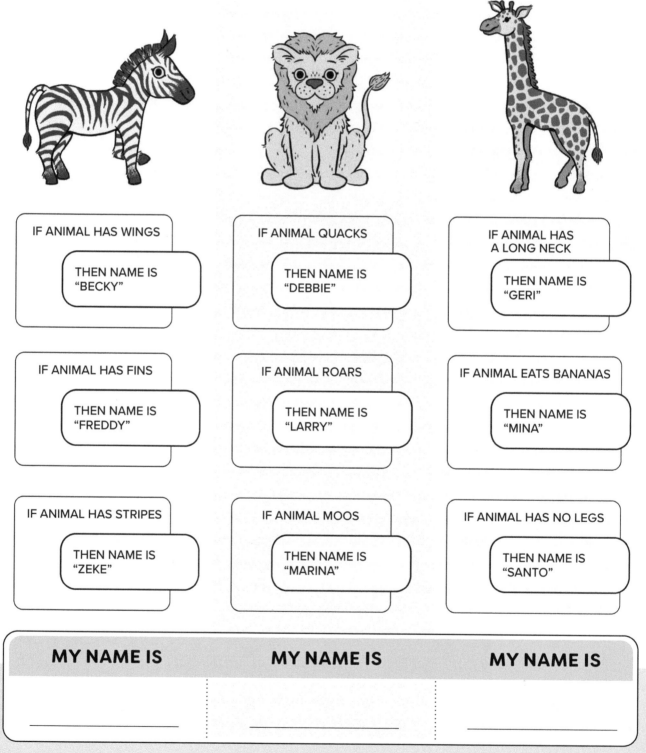

IF ANIMAL HAS WINGS

THEN NAME IS "BECKY"

IF ANIMAL QUACKS

THEN NAME IS "DEBBIE"

IF ANIMAL HAS A LONG NECK

THEN NAME IS "GERI"

IF ANIMAL HAS FINS

THEN NAME IS "FREDDY"

IF ANIMAL ROARS

THEN NAME IS "LARRY"

IF ANIMAL EATS BANANAS

THEN NAME IS "MINA"

IF ANIMAL HAS STRIPES

THEN NAME IS "ZEKE"

IF ANIMAL MOOS

THEN NAME IS "MARINA"

IF ANIMAL HAS NO LEGS

THEN NAME IS "SANTO"

MY NAME IS   **MY NAME IS**   **MY NAME IS**

_____   _____   _____

COLOR BY CONDITIONALS

It's art time! Let's use conditionals to color this picture.

IF NUMBER IS "1" THEN COLOR

IF NUMBER IS "2" THEN COLOR

IF NUMBER IS "3" THEN COLOR

IF NUMBER IS "4" THEN COLOR

IF NUMBER IS "5" THEN COLOR

IF NUMBER IS "6" THEN COLOR

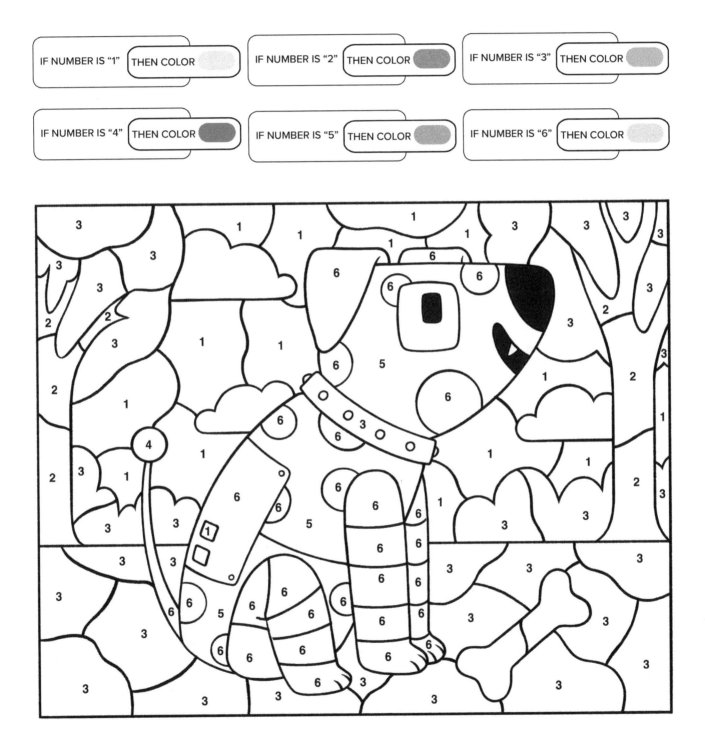

HAT MATCH

Let's play dress-up today. Draw a line from each "then" block to the best hat to match the character you're playing.

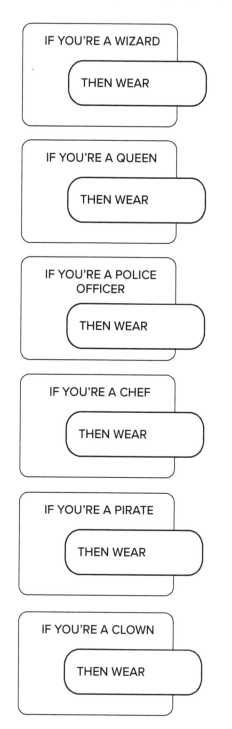

IF YOU'RE A WIZARD

THEN WEAR

IF YOU'RE A QUEEN

THEN WEAR

IF YOU'RE A POLICE OFFICER

THEN WEAR

IF YOU'RE A CHEF

THEN WEAR

IF YOU'RE A PIRATE

THEN WEAR

IF YOU'RE A CLOWN

THEN WEAR

SAY WHAT?

Did you know Spot the Bot can speak different animal languages? Fill in the blanks in the code below with the matching animal sounds.

IF SPEAKING CAT

THEN SAY _____

IF SPEAKING COW

THEN SAY _____

IF SPEAKING FROG

THEN SAY _____

IF SPEAKING DUCK

THEN SAY _____

Now write your own code:

IF SPEAKING _____

THEN SAY _____

IF/THEN, HOP!

Play a jumping race with a fun coding twist.

What You Need:

Painter's tape, yarn, or string
2 or more friends to play
A coin

What You Do:

1. Mark off the starting line and the finish line with the tape, yarn, or string on the floor.

2. Everyone lines up at the starting line. The first person flips the coin. **If** the coin toss is heads, **then** that person takes two hops forward. **If** the coin toss is tails, **then** that person takes one hop back. The coin moves on to the next person.

3. Repeat the coin toss until every player gets a turn. Then start again with the first person. The first player to cross the finish line first wins!

LEVEL UP

Now that you know what conditionals are all about, use this space to write your own if/then code. Try this idea first:

Grab a six-sided die and find a friend to play with. Together, come up with a silly conditional for each number from 1 to 6. For example:

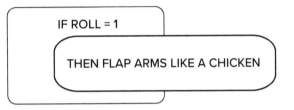

IF ROLL = 1

THEN FLAP ARMS LIKE A CHICKEN

Write the code in the space below, and then take turns playing.

Write your own if/then idea here:

A+ OPTIMIZATION

Optimization is the process of making something as quick and easy as possible. There are lots of ways to solve a problem with code, but some ways are faster and better than others.

Great coders "optimize" their code to make sure it runs smoothly. One way you can optimize your code is by getting rid of steps that you don't need.

Using fewer lines of code can make programs run faster. If you've ever waited a long time for a computer game to start, you know how important that is!

DISH DUTY

A-MAZE-ING RACE

These two rabbits are both hungry and racing to find the carrots. Whoever can get to the carrots in the fewest squares will eat first.

WHICH RABBIT FOUND THE CARROTS FIRST?

BONE DETECTIVE

Which hole will take Spot the Bot to his buried treasure the fastest?

WHICH HOLE SHOULD SPOT USE?

_____

There's more than one path that Spot can take from each hole. Be sure to find the shortest path before choosing your answer.

Pixel loves rock climbing. Which colored path will get her to the top the fastest?
Find the one with the fewest number of handholds.

RED PATH   **GREEN PATH**   **PURPLE PATH**

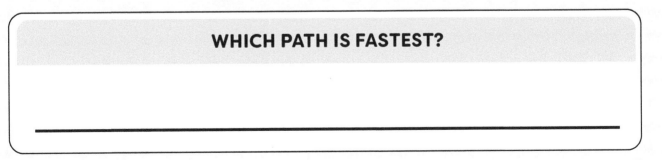

WHICH PATH IS FASTEST?

_____

Help AI optimize packing his picnic basket. Choose the fastest route to collect the food.

Route 1

Basket to sandwich	_____ steps
Sandwich to basket	_____ steps
Basket to cupcakes	_____ steps
Cupcakes to basket	_____ steps
Basket to watermelon	_____ steps
Watermelon to basket	_____ steps
Total	_____ steps

Route 2

Basket to sandwich	_____ steps
Sandwich to cupcakes	_____ steps
Cupcakes to watermelon	_____ steps
Watermelon to basket	_____ steps
Total	_____ steps

WHICH ROUTE IS FASTEST?

_____

Add together all the steps in each route to get the total number of steps.

Help Al collect all of the diamonds in this mine. Use a loop to optimize the code.

CODE 1

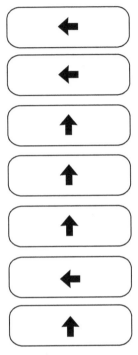

CODE 2

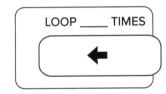

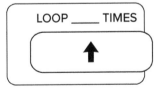

WHICH CODE IS OPTIMIZED?

_____

Here's a fun optimization game that you can play with a friend outdoors. It's a race to see who can carry the most things across the finish line first.

The items below are only a suggestion. Try to pick things that are different shapes, sizes, and weights. Don't choose objects that can break. You'll need two of each item—one for you and one for your friend.

What You Need (2 of each):

Large balls like basketballs or
    soccer balls
Ping-pong balls
Frying pans
Blown-up balloons
Books
Shoes
Empty boxes
Tennis rackets
Empty two-liter bottles
Finish line marker (yarn, a small flag, or
    whatever you have)

What You Do:

1. Make two piles of the same objects: one for you and the other for your friend.
2. When you say, "On your mark, get set, go!" race to see who can carry all of the objects in their pile across the finish line first. Use your optimization skills to take fewer trips.

Now that you know what optimization is all about, use this space to make your own game. Try this idea first:

Make your own optimized drawings. Can you draw a pig using only circles or draw a fish using only triangles? What else can you draw using the fewest shapes and lines possible?

Write your own optimization idea here:

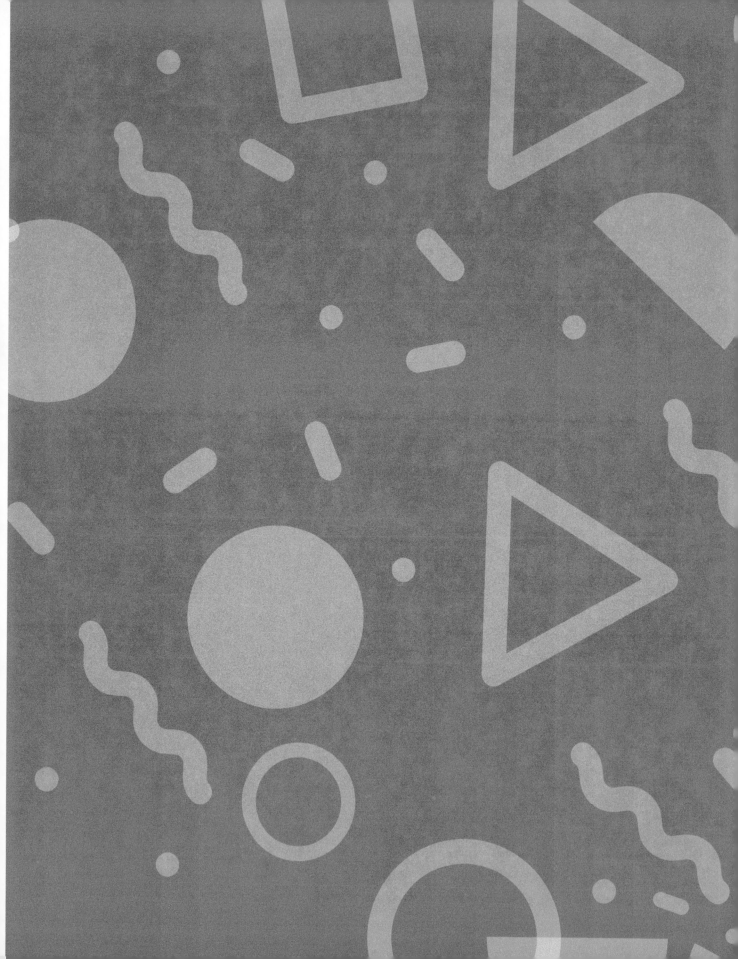

DELIGHTFUL DEBUGGING

Coders call mistakes "bugs."

When you have a bug in your code, your code may not run the way you think it will. Or it may not work at all.

When coders fix bugs, it's called "debugging." To be great at debugging, you need a sharp eye to find things that are out of place. Sometimes you also have to use your head and think logically to figure out why something isn't working.

Debugging can be lots of fun, but it takes practice! The more you know about coding, the better you'll be at finding and fixing all those bugs.

BUG'S BUGS

A good debugger can find small mistakes that other people might miss. See if you can find the three differences between the first and second picture.

Now see if you can find the slug that's not like the other bugs. Circle the one that's different.

BUG IN THE BOTS

Can you find the bug that's hidden in this group of robots?

Bugs can be hard to find, but coders are great at finding things that look out of place.

SNOW BOT SCRAMBLE

Are you good at finding things that are out of order? That skill can be really helpful for debugging. Put these pictures of Bug and his Snow Bot in the right order. Write the correct number in each box.

Spot the Bot has to get to the other side of the dog park. But he can't enter a square that is next to an angry cat. The code below has a bug. Can you find it and fix it?

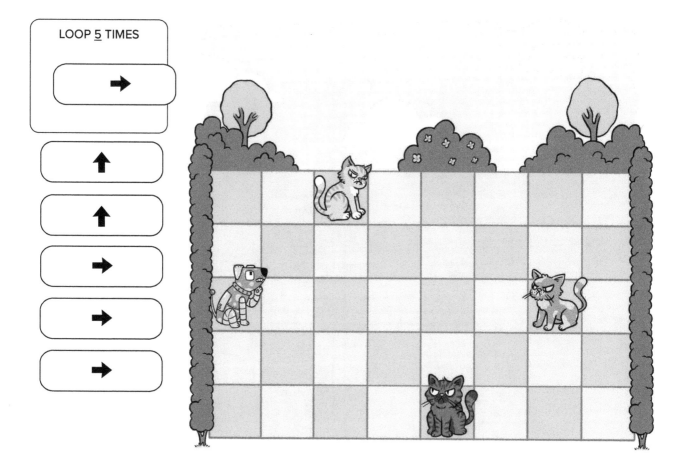

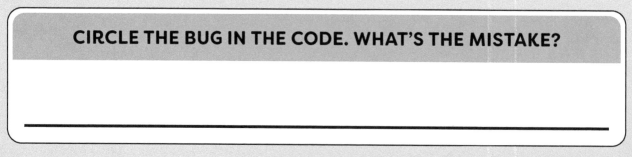

CIRCLE THE BUG IN THE CODE. WHAT'S THE MISTAKE?

_____

LAVA LEAPER

Pixel loves to pretend that the floor of her bedroom is lava. Fix the code below to help her safely jump from rock to rock and get to the other side without touching the lava.

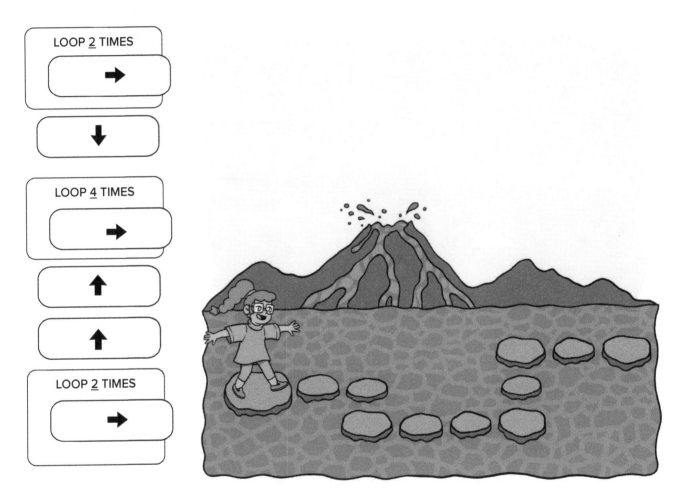

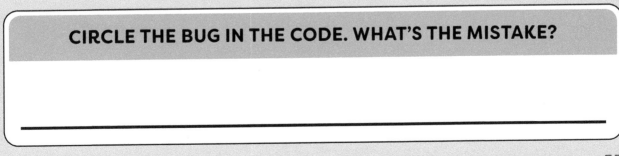

CIRCLE THE BUG IN THE CODE. WHAT'S THE MISTAKE?

COIN CODER

In this game, you'll write down code for a friend to follow. It's a great way to practice algorithms and debugging skills, too.

What You Need:

16 matching coins
Sheet of paper
Pencil

What You Do:

1. Using only arrows (→, ←, ↑, and ↓), write out an algorithm for following a square path that's five coins across and five coins high.

2. Take turns writing the code and following the instructions with your friend. Did you write your code correctly? If not, find the bugs and fix them.

3. Now try writing code to make other things such as numbers or letters. Fix any bugs you find.

YOUR CODE

Now that you know what debugging is all about, use this space to make your own buggy game. Try this idea first:

Write an algorithm explaining how to walk from the front door to the kitchen, but be sure to add a bug or two in the code. See if your friend can figure out how to debug your code.

Write your own buggy game idea here:

VERY VALUABLE VARIABLES

In coding, a variable is something you expect to change.

Think of a variable as being like a box. A box can hold many different things. You can put an apple in the box today and an orange in it tomorrow. What you put inside of the box can change.

If someone asked you today, "How old are you?" your answer might be, "I am six years old." Your age is a variable because you are always growing older. Next year, if someone asked you, "How old are you?" your answer might be, "I am seven years old."

In coder terms, a variable holds a spot for something that can change. A variable always has a *name* and a *value*. In this example, the variable name is your age and the value is the number six.

Can you think of anything else that is always changing?

VARIABLE FAVORITES

Every variable has a name and a value. Look at the name of each variable and fill in the blanks with its value. What are your favorite things? Write down one value for each variable name.

Variable Name   **Value**

Favorite Food   =   _____

Favorite Drink   =   _____

Favorite Color   =   _____

Favorite Animal   =   _____

Favorite Game   =   _____

Favorite Movie   =   _____

Favorite Song   =   _____

Favorite Book   =   _____

You give each variable its value using the equal sign.

Finish drawing the rollercoasters. The first one has been done for you.

hills = 1

hills = 4

hills = 2

hills = 3

Pixel loves to collect things. Help her find how many of each item she has in her collection. Or, in coder terms, figure out the value for each of the variable names.

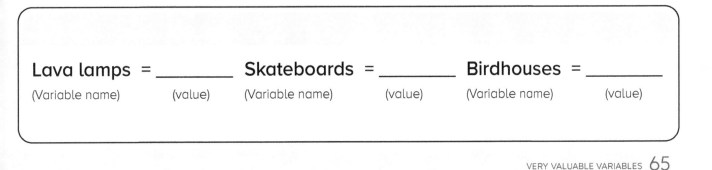

Lava lamps = _____   **Skateboards** = _____   **Birdhouses** = _____
(Variable name)   (value)   (Variable name)   (value)   (Variable name)   (value)

Use the values below to draw each ice cream cone. The first one has been done for you.

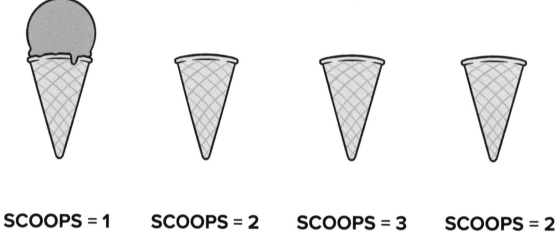

SCOOPS = 1	**SCOOPS = 2**	**SCOOPS = 3**	**SCOOPS = 2**
Color = pink	Color = blue	Color = green	Color = brown

NOW DRAW YOUR FAVORITE ICE CREAM CONE.

SCOOPS = ___

Color = _____

NAME THAT VARIABLE

The pictures in each set look similar, but there is one thing that's different. Fill in the variable name.

THE VARIABLE IS

_____

_____

_____

_____

Remember, variables can change. What changes in each set?

Let's make a paper flower using a variable to pick the color of each petal. If you make more than one flower, every flower will be different!

Cut them out. The circle will be the pistil, or the middle, of your flower, and the oval will be the petal.

2. Use the oval to trace and cut more ovals on all six colors of construction paper. Start with three ovals in each color. You can make more later if needed.

3. Assign a value for each color according to the numbers on the six-sided die. For example:

Number Rolled	Petal Color
1	Red
2	Orange
3	Yellow
4	Green
5	Blue
6	Purple

What You Need:

Pencil
Bottle cap
Construction paper in 6 colors
Scissors
Glue
Six-sided die

What You Do:

1. Trace the bottle cap on a sheet of construction paper and draw a slightly bigger oval on the same sheet.

Now choose your own colors.

Number Rolled	Petal Color
1	
2	
3	
4	
5	
6	

6. Repeat steps 4 and 5 until your flower has six colorful petals. Every flower you make will be unique because the petal colors are a variable.

4. Roll the die and see what number you get. Paste the petal color that matches the number onto the pistil.

5. Now roll the die again to see what the next color should be. Paste the next petal to the right of the one before.

If you don't have colored construction paper, you can use white paper and color the petals instead.

SCAVENGER "SOMETHING" HUNT

Go on a variable scavenger hunt around your house. Use this list of variables and see if you can find "something" that fits as a value.

Variable	Value
Something blue	
Something that smells good	
Something you use to pay people	
Something broken	
Something that falls off trees	
Something green	
Something noisy	
Something shiny	
Something yellow	

Now that you know what variables are all about, use this space to make your own variable activities. Try this idea first:

Make a countdown counter to a special day, such as a birthday or a fun holiday. Count the number of days you have left and put an equal number of pennies, jelly beans, marbles, or other small objects into a jar. To put it in coder terms, the variable name of the jar would be "Number of Days Left" and the value is the amount of objects left in the jar. Each day, you'll take one out. As you get closer to the big day, the number of items in the jar will get smaller and smaller.

Write some of your special dates here. How many days until they arrive?

Special Day	Date

Write your own variable activity idea here:

ANSWER KEY

Awesome Algorithms

....

Code à la Mode [9]

Pie à la mode

Codeo Rodeo [10]

⬇⬇⬅⬅⬆⬆

Word Scramble [11]

Coder Crew Rocks!

Dress Mess [12]

Algorithm 3

Code Connect [13]

A star

Lots of Loops

....

Run the Code [21]

Bug will finish the race.

Laugh-a-Loop [22]

Loop three times, Loop zero times

Hidden Toys [23]

2, 2, 2, 2

Lawn Loops [24]

5 (first loop), 2 (second loop), 4 (third loop), 2 (fourth loop)

Street Repeat [25]

We want traffic lights to loop forever so cars don't crash into each other!

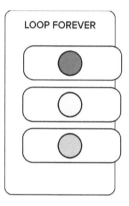

Creative Conditionals

....

Emoji Code [33]

Name Games [34]

Zeke, Larry, Geri

Color by Conditionals [35]

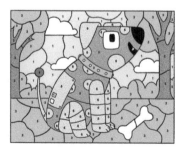

Hat Match [36]

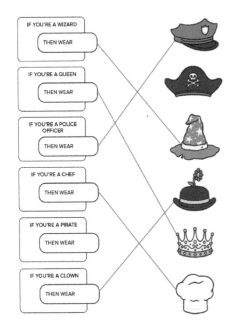

Say What? [37]

Meow, moo, ribbit, quack

A+ Optimization

A-maze-ing Race [43]

The brown rabbit found the carrots first.

Bone Detective [44]

Hole 3

Rock It [45]

The purple path

Pick the Picnic Path [46]

Route 2 is the fastest

Gem Class [47]

Code 1 uses seven blocks. Code 2 uses six blocks.

Code 2 is optimized.

Delightful Debugging

"Spot" the Difference [53]

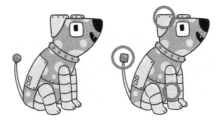

Bug in the Bots [54]

Snow Bot Scramble [55]

3, 2, 1, 4

Mad Cat Dash [56]

There should be four repeats, not five.

Lava Leaper [57]

The second loop should be "3 times."

Very Valuable Variables

Rollercoder [64]

hills = 4

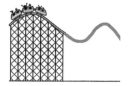

hills = 2

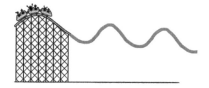

hills = 3

Closet Counting [65]

lava lamps = 3, skateboards = 4, birdhouses = 4

Cone Coding [66]

Name That Variable [67]

Size, number, shape, color

GLOSSARY: CODE WORDS

Algorithm – A set of instructions that are done step-by-step.

Bug – A mistake in code.

Code – Instructions that tell computers what to do.

Command – A single instruction in code.

Computer – Powerful tools that help us use information like numbers, words, sounds, and video.

Conditional – A type of code that causes one thing to happen whenever another thing is true.

Debugging – Fixing a bug (or mistake) in code.

Logic – A type of thinking where you look at many possible answers to a problem and use your head to choose the best one.

Loop – A special kind of code you use when you want to repeat something.

Optimization – Improving your code to get rid of steps you don't need.

Pattern – Something that repeats over and over.

Variable – Code that holds information like words or numbers. Variables have a name and a value.

RESOURCES: KEEP CODING!

Well, that's the end of the book. The next chapter in your coding journey is up to you.

There are many different ways you can keep learning and coding. A few of the best options are listed here.

ScratchJr is an app you can play on Apple and Android phones and tablets. ScratchJr is built for creative minds like yours. You can create animations, tell stories, make games, and more.

Scratch is the "big brother" to ScratchJr. It's designed for kids ages 8 to 16 and uses more advanced coding blocks. Scratch is easy to use, but there's really no limit to what you can do. Scratch allows kids to express themselves creatively and learn from other members of their large online community. Scratch is on the web at Scratch.mit.edu.

Code.org is a fantastic website for learning how to code, no matter your age. Code.org created the Hour of Code event. The Hour of Code happens every year and is the largest education event in the world. They have online lessons for kids from kindergarten through high school.

The Raspberry Pi Foundation is another great resource for young coders. In fact, they're so dedicated to the idea that coding is for everyone that they've invented their own computer that you can buy for about $35. Their website has lessons that teach coding and other fun electronics projects. Their website is RaspberryPi.org.

INDEX

ABOUT THE AUTHOR

Randy Lynn is a creative director and partner at MWB, an advertising and marketing agency, as well as the cofounder of Kids Code Mississippi. He loves teaching kids how to program computers and enjoys speaking to grown-ups about why computer science education is essential. He lives in Ridgeland, Mississippi, with his wife and two children.

CPSIA information can be obtained
at www.ICGtesting.com
Printed in the USA
JSHW060506220223
37977JS00003B/7